GRAND ENTRANCES

Stormy Leather, 1158 Howard Street. Owner Kathy Andrew started the business by designing and sewing leather out of her basement. In 1990, she opened a retail store and a factory-workshop that manufactures all of her products. Designed by Lesley Kushner, the zipper was fabricated from wood and metal by Andrea Stanley.

GRAND ENTRANCES

TERRY HAMBURG · JUDY ERICKSON

VIKING STUDIO

VIKING STUDIO
Published by the Penguin Group
Penguin Putnam Inc., 375 Hudson Street,
New York, New York 10014, U.S.A.

Penguin Books Ltd, 27 Wrights Lane,
London W8 5TZ, England

Penguin Books Australia Ltd, Ringwood,
Victoria, Australia

Penguin Books Canada Ltd, 10 Alcorn Avenue,
Toronto, Ontario, Canada M4V 3B2

Penguin Books (N.Z.) Ltd, 182-90 Wairau Road,
Auckland 10, New Zealand

Penguin Books Ltd, Registered Offices:
Harmondsworth, Middlesex, England

First published in the United States by Viking Studio,
a member of Penguin Putnam Inc.

First Printing, August 2000

10 9 8 7 6 5 4 3 2 1

Copyright © Terry Hamburg and Judy Erickson 2000
All rights reserved.

Library of Congress Catalog Card Number: 00-132169

Book designed by Marilyn Rey
Printed and bound by Dai Nippon Printing Co., Hong Kong, Ltd.

ISBN: 0-670-89215-7

**The authors dedicate this book
to Beverly and Madeleine
whose support was indispensable**

Kearny Video, 1030 Kearny Street.

Soma Caffe, 1601 Howard. Opened in 1982 by photographer Paul
Schultz and Deborah Savage downstairs from their live-work loft
because they couldn't find a good cup of coffee or place to hang out in
the South of Market neighborhood. The outdoor neon logo was bro-
ken so often it was finally replaced by a drawing by Peter Kimack, a
regular customer and storefront artist.

INTRODUCTION

In the fast pace of modern life, with an ever-increasing number of messages competing for our attention, the seductive appeal of the storefront is assuming greater importance to merchants. The days when a typical customer strolled leisurely past a store window and lingered have long since passed. Most people are rushing to work or a luncheon date, taking less than seven seconds to pass a location on foot, according to one estimate, or speeding by in a car, in which case they have perhaps two seconds to notice a merchant's overture, assuming they're not distracted by dialing a cell phone or putting on lipstick.

San Francisco is a city of shopkeepers. In spite of the growing influence of chain-store retailing, The City has maintained its independent entrepreneurial tradition. In his popular tourist-guide book, Arthur Frommer remarks that unlike "department store cities" such as New York and Chicago, the main attraction in San Francisco "lies in small specialty shops boasting a distinctive touch all their own," presenting an array of goods with "individualistic chic and flair."[1] This spirit is exemplified in storefronts—part merchandising, part art, part whimsy—which, like the eyes, can be a window to the soul.

The idea of the storefront as a unique form of communication, devised to create an impression or to convey ambiance, developed slowly. In the nineteenth century, they were sometimes elaborate façades placed on the front of modest structures, and even when personalized served primarily as identification rather than image, designation more than design. After World War I, what we now recognize as the modern age of mass production and mass-media advertising was beginning to define American commerce, and these changes, promoting intense competition among similar products in crowded urban areas, compelled a reexamination of traditional retail practices. "One shop is so like another in its functions, its methods, its merchandise," a study of commercial architecture noted in 1928, "that any opportunity for individual expression would hardly seem to remain."[2] Suddenly, presentation assumed an unprecedented importance. Unusual building design, attention to the aesthetics of layout and decor, fashionable window trimming, and alluring entrances all became subjects of deliberation.

In the 1950s, the shopping center and strip mall came into prominence along with their partner, the chain store, by-products of the expansion of population from cities to suburbs, shaping new metropolitan areas with retail dynamics catering to an automobile-dominated society. Erosion of neighborhood stores and traditional downtown promenades inevitably followed, taking almost a generation to make a significant comeback. The "malling of America" spawned, in the words of the developer who helped to create it, an "entire new industry, one with its own rules, organization and culture,"[3] a culture that promoted uniformity and conventionalism in retail design. The original formula was the department-store model: individual shops in the configuration of a large retail complex, requiring open storefronts with minimal façade or signage, differentiated primarily by merchandise. By the 1980s, there was a clear reaction against this approach, regarded as producing a "boring sameness," prompting a shift to a "street concept" that simulated the atmosphere of old-fashioned neighborhoods. Open façades were downplayed and design regulations relaxed, permitting three-dimensional and neon signs as well as projected storefronts, but freedom of operation was always limited; it was not unusual for a merchant contract to read "storefronts will be controlled by the Landlord both now and in the future."[4]

The pace of shopping-center construction has slowed considerably from its heyday in the 1970s when an average of one thousand new sites were started each year. By the early 1990s commercial design consultants could proclaim "the storefront is back, the sterile shopping-center revolution is over," and the buzzword was "experimental" or "eclectic," a blending and matching of many motifs, the freedom to create a more individual look.[5] However, the

J & D Pet and Vet Supply, 321 Judah Street. This traffic-stopping front was commissioned by the original owner to bring color and excitement to a plain façade. The oil painting on wood, based on a photograph of the owner's Saint Bernard, was done by Van Engel Decorating and Painting, which specializes in faux finishes. The current proprietor inherited the sign and thankfully decided to keep it.

intention and effect of mall merchandising remains a regulated retail image where boldness and non-traditional techniques, especially in storefronts, are inhibited. The chain store, a powerful marketing force in recent years, has found its home in shopping centers and malls as well as traditional commercial areas. By definition, chain merchandising is conservative, cultivating a single image to fit a variety of physical locations and neighborhoods. In terms of storefronts, it is the one-design-fits-all approach. Even within the industry, there are concerns such uniformity may have undesirable consequences. Chain stores reach high levels of success when they "replay their profit formula from city to city, duplicating store design, merchandise selection, and presentation . . . but what will be the long-term effect?" asks a vice-president of The Rouse Company, a major shopping-center builder. "Will the cookie-cutter school of merchandising lead to the elimination of differentiation in regions around the United States?"[6]

San Francisco has followed a somewhat different drummer. It became an important city virtually overnight, transformed from a marshy hamlet of twelve hundred inhabitants in 1848 to a thriving metropolis of a hundred thousand in 1868. The Central Pacific railroad, completed in the same year, would soon carry hundreds of thousands more to the land of dreams where, almost literally, the streets were paved with gold. Bayard Taylor, a correspondent for the *New York Tribune* arriving in the summer of 1848, estimated the population increased from six thousand to thirty thousand in four months, and was astonished at how quickly the infrastructure followed: "Of all the marvelous phases of the present, the growth of San Francisco will tax the belief of the future. . . . Like the magic seed of the Indian juggler which grew, blossomed, and bore fruit before the eyes of his spectators, San Francisco seemed to have accomplished in a day the growth of half a century."[7] Western American cities generally shared more dynamic, less organic patterns of expansion than their Eastern counterparts, and none displayed these characteristics as sharply as gold-rush San Francisco. By 1880, half the population was immigrant, with virtually every national, ethnic, and religious group in America represented. The pace at which newcomers arrived created an environment where toleration of diversity—already a virtue in a nation devoted to common ideals rather than ethnic identity—was reinforced by necessity. The pressure to develop a social order overnight encouraged residents to look to unorthodox solutions. From its earliest days, everything about San Francisco was eclectic and improvisational. People were forced to adapt to immediate circumstances; tradition exercised less influence. The phenomenon had a dark side—the infamous Barbary Coast of taverns, gambling parlors, and houses of ill-repute; an eccentric side, like the improbable Emperor Norton, a wildly popular and acclaimed street character who ruled San Francisco as Emperor of the United States and Protector of Mexico after he lost his fortune and sanity in a grand speculative grain venture; and a dynamic side, providing fertile ground for experimentation in a wide range of activity and expression. Architecture dramatically reflected this spirit. Victorian homes and commercial structures combined Baroque, Georgian, Corinthian, and other motifs, prompting one critic to declare that they "came to pass not by blueprint but by whim."[8] Business in particular was shaped by this high-powered, unpredictable atmosphere. Early San Francisco provided a unique entrepreneurial vacuum, and not only in shipping, banking, and mining. The sudden emergence of great fortunes and the wide distribution of wealth led to an explosion of restaurants, hotels, tailors, milliners, jewelers, cabinetmakers, booksellers—a vast emporium of retail establishments—in order to satisfy a growing appetite for the comforts of civilization amidst a rough-and-tumble frontier cut off from normal channels of supply.

This bustle of small-business enterprise was a reflection of the larger American experience, thriving on what Alexis de Tocqueville, the French aristocrat who chronicled American democracy in the early 1830s, described as "equality of condition, the fundamental fact from which all others seem to be derived." Even in the agrarian paradise of the New World, he observed, people gravitated toward commerce. What he found most remarkable was "not so much the marvelous grandeur of some undertakings, as the innumerable multitude of smaller ones." Ironically, this equality of condition and abundance of opportunity also leads to conformity, in part a consequence of the elimination of caste and class but more profoundly a function of the psychological need to escape the isolation and insecurity of "individualism," a word de Tocqueville recognized as a novel concept: "The power exercised by the mass upon the mind of each individual is extremely great" with the "phantom of public opinion strong enough to chill innovators, and to keep them silent and at a respectful distance," a circumstance "extraordinarily favorable to the stability of opinion."[9] He understood, or at least presaged, that the same forces encouraging the multitude and variety of small enterprises were also planting the seeds for the mass marketing and national merchandising of the next century.

Especially in its early years, practical equality among a diverse population was more widespread in San Francisco than any other urban area. But for various reasons—the physical isolation of The City, its sudden emergence and dynamic growth, the type of people attracted to the West—the second part of de Tocqueville's equation, conformity, never took root as deeply as it did elsewhere. Even as it matured, San Francisco continued to nurture a climate for independence and originality. A 1900 Chamber of Commerce publication acclaimed a city "fed on the intoxicants of a gold rush, developed by an adventurous commerce . . . isolated throughout its turbulent history from the home lands of its diverse people and compelled to the outworking of its own ethical and social standards," welcoming people to a place that "has evolved an individuality and a versatility beyond any other American city. . . . Here is not thralldom to the past, but a trying of all things on their merits, and a searching of every proposal or established institution by the one test: Will it make life happier?"[10] San Francisco's reputation as a culture unique and at times notorious, setting it apart from other American cities, was established early and celebrated by a variety of prominent visitors from Mark Twain to Rudyard Kipling to Oscar Wilde. One could expect to find the unexpected, and experience a measure of freedom perhaps unavailable anywhere else. The bohemian *fin-de-siècle* movement, featuring artists, writers, and bon vivants railing against the "too rigid and oft-times absurd restrictions established by Society,"[11] the Beatnik protest of the 1950s, and the counterculture of the 1960s all found their home in The City. "Innovations in attitude and behavior that would cause uproar in most other American cities," suggests Geoffrey Moorhouse, for many years the chief features editor of *The Guardian*, "are accepted here with hardly a murmur of disapproval. As a result San Francisco is often said to be years ahead of the times—the place to go if you wish to see the lifestyles of the future."[12] Visual art is part of this heritage. A case can be made for a San Francisco "school of art" or at least a distinctive artistic tradition. Thomas Albright, author of *Art in the San Francisco Bay Area: 1945-1980*, speaks of the historical split personality of the area's culture, derived from the mingling of wealth and frontier spirit—on the surface it evokes "a genteel, aristocratic image;

underground, it breeds the volatile rebelliousness that has given birth to the most revolutionary social and cultural movements of the past two generations."[13]

As progressive as it may be today, San Francisco still believes in yesterday. Visitors are surprised at the profusion and variety of Victorian architecture—few other American cities have retained so many early buildings and private residences. Urban modernization in the 1950s sparked a still unresolved conflict between preservationists and those with a more contemporary vision of San Francisco, which became the first large city to challenge the efforts of the freeway builders, initiating the "freeway revolt" that served as a direct model and inspiration for Baltimore, Memphis, Milwaukee, Seattle, and San Antonio, among others. The National Highway Act of 1956, designating generous national matching funds for local road construction, was widely heralded as a bold, forward-looking step to enhance the quality of metropoli-tan life, making cities more convenient and accessible. One official grand plan consisted of ten different freeways crisscrossing San Francisco in every direction, a construction juggernaut that would have had profound repercussions on public buildings, parks, historic sites, retail shops, and residential housing patterns, in some cases virtually uprooting entire neighborhoods. A campaign led by cultural elites and local activists defeated all of the most ambitious proposals, sometimes in mid-tract—the Embarcadero Freeway was already one-third built before it was halted from invading the foot of historic Telegraph Hill and the waterfront, where citizens were in an uproar over the prospect of losing sight of the much-loved Ferry Building. While most cities were lobbying for federal highway funds during this time, San Francisco turned down some sixty million dollars in projects. Later, an even larger array of forces loosely coalesced into the slow-growth and neighborhood preservation movement, culminating in

Café Riggio, 4112 Geary Boulevard. A family-owned restaurant started by John Riggio over twenty years ago, this imposing front was done in 1997 by Jeffrey Skyles, responding to the owner's admiration of murals and his desire to have something that would "stick in the minds of people driving by." A similar mural done by the artist on the same wall in 1991 was the victim of graffiti and subsequently covered. This time he confined the mixed colors to out-of-reach places and used pure primary hues—red, blue, yellow, and shades of green—in the "vulnerable" (i.e. accessible) areas, so if the painting needed a simple touch-up "the owner or dishwasher could run to the hardware store for paint and do it." One of the bells decorating the hat tassels is the fire-alarm bell in disguise.

Proposition M in 1986, the most comprehensive set of development regulations adopted by public vote in a major urban area. An important factor in all these campaigns was the desire to preserve the neighborhood store—not simply nostalgia for the good old days, but a realization of the need to balance the advantages of national retailing with the value of local, community-oriented merchants.

No city combines cosmopolitanism—serving as headquarters for some of the largest banking, insurance, real estate, brokerage and technology-related corporations as well as a center for arts and entertainment—so thoroughly with "provincialism," a commitment to preserve small, unique residential enclaves. San Francisco is a city of neighborhoods, what novelist and resident Herbert Gold calls "America's last great metropolitan village."[14] There was a revival of the concept of neighborhood in urban centers throughout the 1970s, providing access to political power and government grants as well as encouraging historical renovation, and at the same time expanding, especially in San Francisco, from traditional ethnic and class identities to include a variety of communities based on subculture. "Neighborhood" continued to be defined as a commonly recognizable and distinct physical place, usually with its own commercial-retail infrastructure serving the residents in a direct and intimate way. An effort to strengthen these small businesses was a significant part of the slow-growth movement. The focus of the movement was the modification of downtown high-rise construction that came to dominate city politics in the 1980s. *The Transformation of San Francisco*, as the title of a popular book at the time described it, was breathtaking: one major new office building was constructed between 1930 and 1958; in the following two decades fifty-two office towers rose from the downtown nexus. A concerted, well-defined strategy by politicians and corporate interests to redevelop The City was met with steadily increasing opposition. Initiatives to control the heights of new downtown buildings were defeated in the 1970s, although limits were established in most residential areas. It was the linkage of downtown expansion to neighborhood concerns that gave the movement the depth and grass-roots dynamic to succeed. The changes occurring in the financial district were spilling over, directly and indirectly. North Beach and South of Market—areas contiguous to downtown—were obviously impacted, but general problems, such as increased traffic in all parts of The City and on bridges, the lack of parking, accelerating housing prices and rents, and the encroachment of chain merchandising and larger enterprises on neighborhood businesses came to be perceived, accurately or not, as consequences of the effort to redevelop downtown.

The struggle came to a head in hotly contested Proposition M, which codified a moderate-growth vision by establishing standards and procedures for any significant changes to existing architecture and land use. Designed primarily to curb downtown high-rise construc-

tion and perpetuate historic architecture in the neighborhoods, the determination to protect small retail business was a strong motivating force in the campaign. The opening provision of Proposition M states: "That existing neighborhood-serving retail uses be preserved and enhanced and future opportunities for residential employment in and ownership of such businesses be enhanced." Although not specifically designating small as opposed to chain or large-scale stores, the intent and practical effect of the policy was to promote the former. "Soon you may have to go to San Jose to get your shoes repaired," declared a pro-M statement appearing in the official voter's election guidebook. "Neighborhood serving merchants, community meeting places, and small employers are being driven out of our town by direct high-rise expansion, or by its effects on all our neighborhoods—higher rents, denser traffic, neighborhood turnover, office conversions, and parking problems." This defense of local communities contributed to the expansion of independent enterprises—and the imaginative storefronts that announce their presence.

In the post-Proposition M era, San Francisco remains in the forefront of the effort to modify the influence of national merchandising, and hardly a week goes by without a neighborhood group protesting the loss of local businesses and stores. In the 1999 municipal elections, a candidate accused the mayor of presiding over a "chain-store invasion," warning that The City "is losing the character of its neighborhoods and its neighborhood shopping districts, and once it is lost, it will never, ever be recovered." He proposed tightening the zoning requirements to regulate "formula businesses," which were defined as those that promote standardized decor, services, architecture, and signs.[15] In spite of this "invasion," which most critics concede also provides service and choice to consumers, it is an irony and a tribute to the small merchant in San Francisco that in recent years rather than downtown business and shopping malls diminishing neighborhood stores, there has been a reverse osmosis, with the flair and whimsy of these stores influencing how merchants on Market Street or the popular tourist complexes, such as the Embarcadaro or Fisherman's Wharf, present themselves to the public.

The proliferation of imaginative storefronts began in San Francisco in the late 1980s. South of downtown, known as South of Market or Soma, was the last part of the small forty-nine-square-mile metropolis where significant new retail development could occur. Currently, in the midst of an unprecedented residential and commercial building boom, this long-neglected industrial/warehouse area began its transformation in the 1970s, led by New Wave music clubs and artists in search of work space. Outlet-distribution stores attracted by larger floor plans and lower rents established a presence, and soon more modest ventures were finding their way to Soma. From this last group of urban pioneers, as well as established small businesses in the area, the storefront revolution emerged. The Loma Prieta earthquake of 1989 served as

TMR, 219 9th Street. The owner wanted a dramatic image for his restaurant-equipment outlet, so he commissioned Peter Kimack, who lives in the neighborhood and has done striking fronts for other businesses in San Francisco. The mural was based on a poster by Leonetto Cappiello.

both a setback and an opportunity. Business in Soma was particularly hard hit because of the disruption of traffic over the Bay Bridge, the main artery connecting San Francisco to the East Bay, and during this period merchants were more responsive to unusual storefronts in the hope of stimulating sales. Soma is compared to the Soho district of New York City, which has a similar assortment of late-night music, bars, restaurants, galleries, artist studios, and small shops. Soho is a collection of neighborhoods characterized in part by brick buildings and brownstones, as well as factories and warehouses of the late nineteenth century that often feature ornate embellishments or grandiose façades. Storefronts in Soho adapt to the existing architecture. In contrast, the most common structure

in Soma is squat, utilitarian, sometimes detached, having little adornment, and constructed with masonite or concrete—a blank canvas waiting to be filled. The storefront phenomenon gradually appeared in all sections of The City, concentrated initially in the Haight-Ashbury, Mission Dolores, and Castro neighborhoods, areas regarded as artistic, trendy, or pace-setting.

The confluence of art and commerce is tenuous—art doesn't care what commerce does and commerce doesn't care what art does—but their intersection in retail merchandising has long been established, with the storefront receiving less attention than the interior. Designing an entrance façade is at the same time both simple and difficult to achieve, and execution can fall short of expectation.

Martin Pegler, Professor of Store Planning and Visual Merchandising at the Fashion Institute of Technology in New York, compares a storefront to the overture of a Broadway musical: "It is the first impression you get of the sound, melodies and tempo you are about to enjoy," a collage "to create the essence of what lies beyond."[16] One design consultant urges a merchant to "create drama, excitement and the promise that dreams will be fulfilled. As a proscenium sets the stage for the play, the storefront sets the stage for the sale."[17] These are challenging blueprints, perhaps impossible to fulfill; in the end, professional designers tend to be conservative, urging "a simple and classic approach." The common advice is to be "more neutral than strong . . . sell the product, not the storefront."[18] In San Francisco, storefronts have gone beyond traditional ideas and reached for the impossible, encompassing powerful use of art and symbolism.

Occasionally, a storefront was constructed by an owner who had little or no experience in art or industrial design, and the results can be accomplished and striking. However, most were produced by individuals contracted by merchants to execute a specific façade. San Francisco has a large indigenous community of visual artists—painters, muralists, illustrators, graphic designers, restoration experts, sculptors, fabricators, faux-surface specialists—prepared to take on such commercial projects not only for financial support but also to express their talent and vision. Storefront design in San Francisco has assumed the status of an art form in its own right. These independent artists, ranging from formally trained to completely self-taught—some working entirely freelance, others with more regular and established commissions—do not confine their work to or necessarily specialize in storefront design; the assignments are another chance, often a unique challenge, to practice or expand their craft.

Peter Kimack, responsible for some of the most dramatic storefronts, has taken a variety of artistic jobs in San Francisco since the 1960s, when he was actively involved in the design of psychedelic posters. Most of his work is for individuals or small enterprises coming to him through reputation and word-of-mouth; his imagery and lettering are rendered freehand, a practice typical of the artists who do these storefronts.

Jeffrey Skyles, a graduate of the Academy of Art College in San Francisco with a degree in fine arts and illustration, in charge of restoring the historic Raphael Theatre in San Raphael, and currently commissioned to do murals for the new San Francisco Giants stadium—enjoys the opportunity to do storefront work, especially when it involves figural painting. He points out that artists seldom make a living at the discipline in which they were trained, and must be versatile and self-motivated if they wish to survive as independents.

One can have a serendipitous introduction to the genre. Jon Weiss, with some formal art-institute training but largely self-taught, decided to begin doing murals, which quickly expanded to storefronts, one morning over breakfast after he overheard the restaurant owner casually remark that an interior wall painting would add much-needed decoration to the business. An "I can do that" response launched his career.

Those who utilize this independent pool of talent are often prepared to give artists considerable latitude, sometimes presenting a *tabula rasa* and vague instructions to do something "exciting" that will attract attention. When the owner of a restaurant in a converted commercial garage wanted to spruce up the drab, peeling olive-green front, she found Andy Junge, who specializes in portraiture and still life, eager to accept a challenge to "translate" the interior decor of paintings inspired by Hieronymus Bosch, a 15th-century artist known for his evocative allegorical imagery, to the thirty-foot-tall exterior. The result, completed by a crew of artists perched on scaffolds for weeks, was a wild chromatic collage of forms and imagery. Junge was grateful to be granted such artistic freedom, describing San Francisco, his adopted home, as a city of "arts patronage."

San Francisco has been called the mural capital of the world. Muralism began its modern development in the late 1960s and early 1970s as "community-based" wall art depicting political and cultural themes. The artists were usually connected to or part of the community, underwritten by government bodies or foundations, and careful to consult grass-roots organizations about content and location. As political activism subsided and public funding lessened, murals were done more as general decorative art for a variety of public and private spaces. This development pulled the medium into the mainstream, sometimes supported by corporations and other private institutions or done on the initiative of artists whose primary motivation was self-expression. Occasionally, community-based work is conceived on buildings where businesses are located, but muralism as an art form has been widely applied to storefronts, which provide a city-wide canvas, and many of the artists engaged in that work, whether or not they describe themselves as muralists, are influenced in some degree by the historic-mural movement. It was a natural transition for dramatic, colorful wall painting to become fashionable storefront identification in a city that had for decades sponsored and celebrated such activity. The owner of an Internet coffee house wanted to paint the one-hundred-foot side of his building with a bold logo and store name, but The City rejected it as exceeding signage limitations; presented in the same form and redefined as a

Right. ZA Spot 4 Pizza, 371 11th Street. Designed and painted by Andy Junge along with Claran Foley and friends, who spent six weeks on a scaffold completing the mural. The restaurant owner wanted to make the drab, flat front of what was originally a commercial garage "jump out," especially to passing motorists.

mural, it was immediately approved. The expansion of storefronts in the 1990s has led to the muralization of San Francisco.

There are few companies that do storefront imagery and lettering by hand or devote time to creative brainstorming; the industry is more and more influenced by digital and computer technology. In the forefront of those leaning against this trend are Barry Foreman and Kat Wilson, who began a collaboration in 1990 called Back to the Drawing Board, specializing in sidewalk, hanging, and three-dimensional signage and façades. Kat graduated from the Academy of Art College in San Francisco majoring in illustration; Barry had a brief stint as an industrial-arts teacher. About one-quarter of their clients have a clear idea of what they want, occasionally a particular image; however, most come with only a general desire to do something different or eye-catching. Barry and Kat welcome and elicit ideas, but will decline a job if their artistic freedom is too limited. They prefer to work for small, independent merchants rather than chain stores or large companies where the standard operating procedure is decision by committee, and a storefront can turn into a "Frankenstein monster" or the "lowest common denominator." They once developed an elaborate Alice in Wonderland Mad Hatter Coffee Party motif for a string of doughnut shops, only to have it watered down to Mr. Egg Man by the board of directors to the dismay and apology of the hapless owner who loved the original idea.

When Barry began his work in 1984, traditional storefronts were the norm and it was difficult to convince merchants to try something innovative: "When I asked what they wanted they would usually give me a blank look or a shrug and say 'you know, some kind of identifying sign,' drawing a rectangle in the air with their fingers. And that's what I saw all around town, the generic rectangle." A storefront is more than identification, he suggested, it's the way to entice customers: "You have to grab their attention and you may have only one chance—be conspicuous." This argument has a special appeal to small merchants in competitive marketplaces unable to maintain expensive media budgets or survive on reputation.

After they consult with a client, Kat will carefully draw the design to provide an accurate representation of the finished storefront down to the smallest detail. Kat's major influences are Norman Rockwell's character studies, the colors of Maxfield Parrish, and Salvador Dali for imagery; add Barry's lifelong love affair with Walt Disney and you have a palette eclectic enough to satisfy any taste. The construction techniques have evolved over the years, improving on quality and endurance of materials and color, including the use of fiberglass and foam and encompassing three-dimensional and motorized products. Most of the hanging and sidewalk signs are made of wood with internal metal skeletons, then oil-painted twice over an acrylic base, which imparts a glowing and uniform color, and is less susceptible to fading. Their work has always been characterized by whimsy and color. Color is important. "Your sight," Kat explains, "especially in situations where time is limited, such as passing by in a car, is attracted immediately to the most vivid color and then absorbs the rest of the picture. We try to establish this color magnet and formulate the design around it." In storefront design language it is a "visual stopper." Back to the Drawing Board no longer has to twist arms to get merchants to consider unusual designs. As more embrace innovation, others are willing to take risks. The storefront movement has a cumulative, snowball effect.

There is an effort to make a storefront fit the personality of the building and neighborhood, a practice widespread in The City, going beyond minimum zoning requirements. In the process of working on an idea, Barry and Kat photograph the building as well as the structures to the left and right, taking into account how the new façade will impact the street and immediate area, for what is appropriate in one location may not be in another. The architecture of San Francisco, which is primarily wood and stucco, is more amenable to unconventional storefronts than the brick and stone architecture of the Midwest and East where bold colorful façades can be intrusive both physically and aesthetically. There is also greater durability of signage on the temperate West coast. In San Francisco, the ubiquitous Victorians have been uniquely adapted to the late-twentieth century, facilitating the wave of new storefronts. When restoration fever hit in the 1970s, many of these classic structures were not returned to historically accurate condition; they were, in fact, reinvented to fit contemporary visions. Painting The City with pots of color was a reflection of San Francisco's non-traditional traditionalism. The abundance of Victorians permitted a response of this magnitude. In a small town or a city with limited old architecture, the drive for restoration might be more faithful, inhibiting such robust decoration, but in an area abounding in older buildings there was room for both purity and experimentation. The "Painted Ladies" phenomenon set the stage—literally—for the storefronts that followed, not simply by creating the artistic climate for such innovation, but by establishing a chromatic cityscape that both inspired and demanded an equal vibrancy from its businesses, many of which found their homes in those structures.

Artistic trends appear to unfold automatically or spontaneously, and to some extent they do—movements, after all, are the result of individuals "catching fire" in the same place at the same time. But San Francisco is an environment, not a vacuum, and its special history and culture create the conditions where storefront art can flourish. When he arrived in The City, Barry Foreman's first impression was that the storefronts failed to reflect the diversity and vitality he saw all around him. The time for change was at hand. Imaginative groups of artists and merchants are continually at work remaking the face of San Francisco.

Alfred Schilling Restaurant, 1695 Market Street. Peter Kimack's concept and design were inspired by an Egyptian goddess.

Overleaf. Grooves, 1797 Market Street. In 1996, Ray and Joan Anderson opened this record store specializing in unusual and vintage LP's. Ray designed and created the storefront. "Groove" was a record company in the 1950s, and the colored records decorating the windows are all originals from the 1950s through the 1970s. The one-story building was restored to its original form after the 1906 earthquake.

DETECT ALL
SECURITY
(60_) 286-2527

GR

GRo

1795

CLOSED

1
7
9
7

GROOVES
Vinyl Attractions

TO PLAY
BETTER BASEBALL

Western Tire Sales, 610 Bryant Street. The owner wanted a storefront that would attract attention on a busy South of Market thoroughfare. Back to the Drawing Board came up with this difficult-to-miss grease monkey in 1993.

S F Magnetz, 106 Powell Street. The store and sign are now gone; sad, for it was a landmark.

Tires Plus, 368 11th Street. Bored with an unadorned façade in an industrial/warehouse area south of downtown, the owner commissioned Peter Kimack to spruce up the building in an effort to stimulate business. The dramatic front helped maintain sales following the Loma Prieta earthquake of 1989.

Qube Auto Body, 765 Harrison Street. Owner Bob Mendez, known since high school for his perfect-condition 1959 Corvette, saw his prized possession burn almost beyond recognition in a fire that destroyed his uninsured body shop. In the search for parts to rebuild the car, he accumulated enough to erect a replica above the entrance of his new auto-body business, complete with neon accents. The perfectly restored Corvette sits covered in a corner of the shop and is promised to a daughter, who is eagerly awaiting her sixteenth birthday.

Franklin Auto Body, 24 Franklin Street. Installed eight years ago by owner Issa Aho after his existing sign was the victim of graffiti, this storefront was built with the remnants of a complete Jaguar body he purchased from a junkyard. A special permit was needed to hang the car, the license number of which is the telephone number of the store. The headlights work.

The Typewritorium, 1234 Folsom Street. Third-generation owner Eric Bickel decided to remodel his façade, damaged in the Loma Prieta earthquake of 1989. The existing business identification was a funky square-fluorescent 3' by 6' aluminum sign. Impressed by the work Back to the Drawing Board did for Weiss Welding across the street, Mr. Bickel requested a livelier image for his store, and ended up, to his surprise and delight, with a sculpture winding its way across the building front.

Weiss Welding, 1237 Folsom Street. The business was begun in 1934 and has been at the present location since 1938, using a man in a welder's hat as a general logo since the end of World War II. Third-generation owner Bill Weiss does metal work for Back to the Drawing Board, who suggested an update of the old symbol with a marooned alien craft getting "out of this world" repair by Mr. Welder in a spaceman outfit. The idea was a little too radical for the business that finally settled on a more colorful version of its traditional logo.

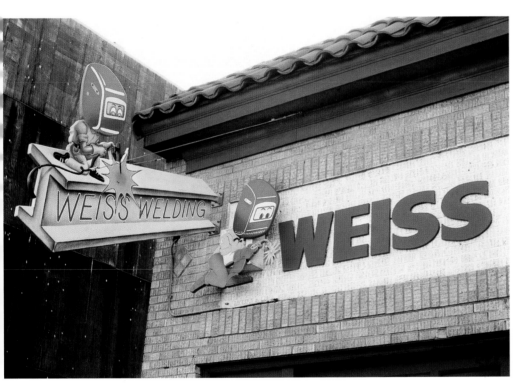

Overleaf. Buffalo Whole Foods, 598 Castro Street. The mural was designed by Luiz Da Rosa and David Seibold of Art Lick Gallery in 1990, and inherited by the current proprietor, who acquired the store three years ago. The side of the structure was damaged in the Loma Prieta earthquake of 1989; rather than fully restore the wall, the building owner decided on artwork that would incorporate any damage, and at the same time complement the existing business. Faux bricks along the border match the original bricks.

POSITIVELY HAIGHT STREET

Holy Cow, 1535 Folsom Street. The cow, constructed of "a plaster-like material" over a wire-mesh skeleton cage, was purchased at a swap meet in 1987 and came with the South of Market bar when owner Jeff Thompson bought it two years ago. A neon halo was added and then removed when a neighbor complained the light interfered with his sleep. An attempt to steal the cow apparently proved overwhelming; abandoned in an alley, it needed restoration. At some point an employee added the ring to the udder. Mr. Thompson liked the mystery of having a cow displayed above his bar and dance club, but he has recently added a few notes of music to the building façade to give a hint of what lies inside.

This mural decorates the building above the New Sun Hong Kong Restaurant, Columbus Avenue and Broadway, in a neighborhood known for its nightlife. Done by Mirage, Inc., in 1988.

Left. Positively Haight Street, 1400 Haight Street. One block from historic Haight-Ashbury, this counter-culture general store was opened in 1996 and moved around the corner the following year. The colorful imagery was designed by Tony Machado, a muralist in San Francisco since 1971 who has done both public and commercial projects, including the Bay Area Rapid Transit (BART) station at Mission and 24th Streets. Along with his daughter, Malia, he painted this business façade at the urging of friend and store owner Jim Preston. It represents the Haight Street community, incorporating some of the people who frequent this popular "hang-out" corner.

The Coffee Net, 744 Harrison Street. The 100-foot-long logo on this coffee house, with Internet access at the tables, was conceived and painted by co-owner Richard Thomas. The design was originally rejected by zoning authorities because it exceeded signage limitations. Thomas's architect resubmitted the same idea and redefined it as a mural, which was approved. The image is a take-off on the Microsoft Flying Toaster screensaver.

Former Hugo Apartments, 6th and Howard Streets. Designed in 1997 by Brian Goggin, who lived in the neighborhood for years, with the help of seventy-five volunteer sculptors and artists. Only after a long search and many rejections was he able to obtain this vacant South of Market building, which originally housed street-level retail stores and a jazz club, to incorporate his installation art project entitled *Defenestration,* meaning "throwing a thing or person out of a window." He describes the sculpture as a contemporary caveman painting with urban objects representing the animals that previously roamed the range.

Port Café, 3499 16th Street. The owner, who specializes in Cuban cuisine and decorates the interior with native costumes and music albums, requested a façade that didn't display food. Back to the Drawing Board, inspired by Carmen Miranda and Ricky Ricardo, produced the undulating silverware intended to suggest that the meals here "dance in your mouth."

De Vera, 580 Sutter Street. The contemporary hand-blown glass pieces are of Italian, Austrian, and American origin. All of the window displays are done by owner Federico de Vera, who was trained as an architect. He takes care to balance the colors in order not to overwhelm or distract the observer.

Overleaf. This mural covers the entire side of the building containing the OSAS Market, 4900 3rd Street. Entitled *Tuzari Watu/We are a Beautiful People,* it was painted by Brooke Fancher in 1987.

33

FINNEGANS

ACE
SIGNS

·WAKE·

EST. 1976

Left. Finnegans Wake, 937 Cole Street. The picture originally appeared on T-shirts for the tavern's 1976 opening, which were done by Dennis Larkins, who designed sets for the Grateful Dead and other rock groups as well as the San Francisco Opera. Maurine Rasumussen painted the hanging sign in 1989 with owner Tom Frenkel's body shown lying on the bar.

Gangway, 84 Larkin Street. San Franciscans are fond of this sculptural bar sign that was created by Wes Haug in 1996.

Animal Farm, 5601 Mission Street. The mural, which extends along the entire side of the building, a short city block, was the idea of veterinarian Noah Stroe, who contemplated for years doing something to cover an unadorned and discolored wall. He was able to convince handyman Crecensino Contreras to bring his long-nurtured Noah's Ark vision to life: "Mexicans are the greatest muralists in the world, would you try one for me?" Dr. Stroe holding a cat in the window was the result of a conspiracy between his wife and the artist. "I returned from lunch and I discovered myself on the wall. I asked that it be removed, but Señor Contreras refused."

Café Mozart, 708 Bush Street. The restaurant has been at this location for twenty-two years; the name inspired by owner Fred Fahrni's
lifelong love affair with Mozart's music. The restaurateur specializes
in French and California dishes, for "we could not survive in San
Francisco serving German food."

A Clean Well-Lighted Place for Books, 601 Van Ness Avenue.
Owner Neal Sofman named the bookstore after a short story by
Ernest Hemingway.

Bound Together Anarchist Bookstore, 1369 Haight Street. Designed and painted in 1994 by Susan Greene, a prominent San Francisco muralist. Owned and operated by a collective, the book store has been at its present location since 1983. The content of the mural was determined by members of the collective in conjunction with the artist, and features prominent North American anarchists along with a few local friends and associates.

Overleaf. SomArts Cultural Center, 934 Brannan Street. This cultural-arts center features a variety of changing exhibits, specializing in local artists. The façade, entitled *Artifact,* symbolizes many cultures and was completed in acrylic on concrete in 1990 by well-known muralist Johanna Poethig, who has adorned other parts of The City and Los Angeles.

SomArts

SomArts
CULTURAL CENTER

934 BRANNAN ST.

SOUTH OF MARKET · SOMAR · CULTURAL CENTER

Vino & Cucina Trattoria, 489 3rd Street. The giant tomato was hanging from the restaurant when the present owner bought the business.

Left. Dovre Club, in The Women's Building at Lapidge and 18th Streets; since moved to 1498 Valencia Street. The Women's Building mural was done by Juana Alicia, Miranda Bergman, Edythe Boone, Susan Cervantes, Meera Desai, Yvonne Littleton, and Irene Perez.

House of Magic, 2025 Chestnut Street. This colorful storefront depicting the merchandise inside has decorated the magic shop since its opening in 1967, changing in some detail every few years. The work is done and redone by Bob Lippi Signs.

The Ocularium, 2336 Chestnut Street. Owner Bob Knopp, who opened the business in 1975, wanted an antique-looking sign and name. In the past, opticians were called oculists and commonly had eyeglasses as part of their store signs. Searching through old San Francisco phone books, Knopp discovered a store called The Ocularium. The eyeglasses were based on a 1906 picture. The restored Art Deco building houses the Presidio Movie Theatre.

Bagdad Cafe, 2295 Market Street. The restaurant was named after a movie. Owner George Maumer wanted a desert image, so Back to the Drawing Board recommended a cactus. Unable to create an appropriate face—"It's easy to put an expression on a hot dog or a pickle; it just didn't look right on a cactus"—they gave it sunglasses, a large hat, and a bandanna to create character.

The Attic, 2445 Taraval Avenue. Immigrating from Hungary as a young man with twenty dollars in his pocket, owner George Tabak, described as the last of the secondhand men, drifted into the antiques business after he sold some junk from his basement at the now defunct Cow Palace Flea Market in San Francisco, taking in more money in one morning than he made in a day as a tool-and-die maker. He became "braver and braver," eventually quitting his job and opening a small shop. He has been at the present location since 1973. The awning and signage were designed by the owner and date from 1978.

Right. Scairy Hairy Toy Cº, 3804 17th Street. Until 1998, this gallery produced original toys, prints, and character dolls in collaboration with comic-book artists and others, and was then transformed itself into Kitty Katty's, a gallery featuring a variety of items made by owner Flower Frankenstein, who was part of the previous enterprise. The Scairy Hairy logo was created by Bruce Helvitz.

SCAIRY HAIRY
TOY Co

Firefly Restaurant, 4288 24th Street. Searching desperately for a name for their newly acquired restaurant, one of the owners asked his cousin to come up with fond memories from her childhood as an inspiration, and the Firefly was born. The large steel insect with Plexiglas wings was done in 1993 by William Wareham, a local sculptor whose work graces other storefronts. He has exhibited and sold sculpture in the Bay Area for thirty years and currently teaches at the Academy of Art College in San Francisco.

Left. Lisa Violetto Designs, 425 Brannan Street. Back to the Drawing Board picked out items from this women's-accessory store, which designs and makes handbags and scarves, so sprightfully illustrated on the sign.

Celebrate Your Smile!, 1794 San Jose Avenue. This dental practice wanted to attract more children while keeping its adult clientele. Created by Back to the Drawing Board, the toothy chorus line was dictated by the long narrow width of the space available for signage. Each of the dancing teeth was made separately, and they interlock like a jigsaw puzzle.

Jennifer Crandall, D. D. S., 2920 Lyon Street. Dr. Crandall moved from a professional building to her current location in a Victorian nestled in a mainly residential neighborhood across the street from a park. She wanted to identify herself clearly as a dentist yet fit into the ambiance of the surrounding architecture which included Liverpool Lil's, an old-fashioned-looking pub. The tooth was inspired by English signs of the nineteenth century. She brainstormed with artist Nicolai Larsen, one of her patients. who fabricated the sign from styrene, foam, wood, and fiberglass, and finished it with enamel paints. Nicolai Larsen attended the San Francisco Art Institute and does sign painting as well as sculpture and decoration for storefronts.

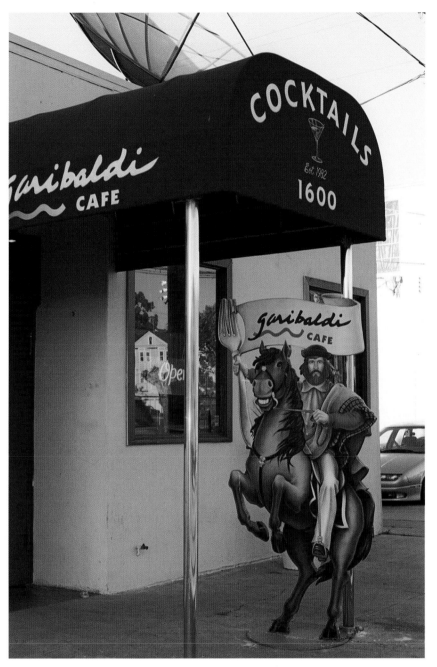

Garibaldi Cafe, 1600 17th Street. The restaurant is named after Giuseppe Garibaldi, the Italian general who led the unification of Italy in the nineteenth century. Back to the Drawing Board's Garibaldi is based on an old painting. The horse was constructed rearing up in order to conform to the permitted width for sidewalk signage. Like all such work by the design company, the sign contains a metal skeleton under the wood and is attached to a heavy, round steel base.

Overleaf. C & S Designs, 99 Missouri Street. This block-long mural was done in 1997 by Urban Street Gallery specifically for C & S, which has closed.

TONY

THE GREAT
SF
DELI CO.

Leon's Bar-B-Que, 2800 Sloat Boulevard. The portrayal of the owner riding a sausage was done by Back to the Drawing Board.

Holey Bagel, 1206 Masonic Avenue. The store is now named Manhattan Bagel, which has removed the sign created by Back to the Drawing Board.

Left. The Great SF Deli Co., 1526 California Street. This restaurant is located on a street with a cable-car line, so Back to the Drawing Board perched the owner on top of a cable car.

R. Matteucci Jewelry, 450 Columbus Avenue. This family business was opened 113 years ago a few blocks from its current location, where it has been since 1977. The magnificent cast-iron Seth Thomas clock was installed in 1908 and moved with the store. When the original owner of the clock died, it mysteriously stopped and the owner's son, a collector and repairman, was unable to fix it. One week later, it miraculously restarted. A similar Seth Thomas clock in San Diego is said to have behaved exactly the same way when its owner died. Over the years the clock survived mishaps, including a Fourth of July stray bullet that shattered the glass and dial, as well as the theft of the works, which brought the thieves twenty-nine dollars in scrap and led to the installation of an electric movement. But in October 1999, a delivery truck backing into a rare North Beach parking space toppled the landmark, and at this point its resurrection is still in doubt. "People came pouring out of offices and cafés along Columbus, some near tears, as if they had come upon someone dying," the *San Francisco Chronicle* reported. The truck driver "looked like he was going to cry."

Ultimate Yogurt & More, 495 Castro Street. The owners, David and Ellie Gross, wanted to show that they were not your typical yogurt store. "Health, fruit, cornucopia," were the "marching orders" to the architect. The sign was made with Styrofoam. They have an identical business in a shopping mall but are prevented from using the cone on the storefront; instead they must display their name in the same printed style as everyone else. Comments Mr. Gross: "It's hard for a merchant to differentiate himself in a mall."

Overleaf. Artesanias Cuscatlan, 3021 24th Street. This bright display now houses the Mission Neighborhood Center. The mural, a community-based art project inspired by Huichol Indian Yarn painting, was done by Susan Cervantes and others in 1991.

Bottom of the Hill, 1233 17th Street. The neon sign was made in 1991 when the business changed owners. A restaurant or bar called Bottom of the Hill has been in the location for thirty years. The cityscape design is used throughout the interior.

Blown Away, 583 Haight Street. The owner inherited the storefront when she bought this hair-styling business five years ago.

Cards and Comics Central, now at 5522 Geary Boulevard. Recently moved to a new address two blocks away, the owner was unable to hang the sign because of an all-glass façade. Barry Foreman of Back to the Drawing Board got permission from Spiderman-creator Stan Lee to use the image. The artist advised him "to keep thy spiderwebs untangled."

Cinch, 1723 Polk Street. The bar front was done in 1988 by Back to the Drawing Board. The Western motif was suggested by the old wooden front of the building.

Caldwell Lumber, 195 Bayshore Boulevard. Recently, employees arriving at work in the morning found the heavy cast-iron tub and Betty, the mannequin, lying on the floor, victim of a fall caused by dry rot. The tub survived intact, but not Betty; one plan is to resurrect the logo, a well-known landmark, with a new bather. The owner is also contemplating something completely different, including a rescue of the giant dachshund head from the last Doggie Diner in San Francisco, should it ever be removed from its location near the City Zoo.

1st Historically Recorded Hardware Store

THE STORY OF COLE HARDWARE

COLE

Friendliest Service

Since the Days of the Gold Rush....

Cole Hardware, 956 Cole Street. *The Story of Cole Hardware,* an ambitious mural tracing the "history" of the hardware store from prehistoric times into the future, was the brainstorm of owner Rick Karp, who hired Back to the Drawing Board to elaborate the story line and imagery. The owner wanted to suggest a friendly, engaging atmosphere and convey the message that the store had been a part of the Cole Valley neighborhood for many years and would continue to serve the community in the future.

Overleaf. O'Farrell Theatre, 895 O'Farrell Street. The owners, Jim and Art Mitchell, commissioned this block-long mural on the side and back of the building, with animals and endangered marine species as a theme, in an effort to control a graffiti problem. Painted by Lou Silva, Juan Karlos, Gary W. Graham, and Edgar Monroe.

O'Farrell T[...]

"THE PLACE TO GO IN S[...]
ALL NEW PRIVATE[...]
GET TO KNOW THE[...]
SUZI SUZUKI AND [...]
"ON YOUR LAP" APRIL[...]
ULTRA ROOM PRIVATE[...]
CONTINUOUS NUDE S[...]
INTERNET WWW. OFA[...]

Beep's Burgers, 1051 Ocean Avenue. The neon sign is from 1963, a period when America was deeply committed to the "space race."

Donuts by All Star, Steiner and Chestnut Streets. The neon sign has been hanging in front of the shop since its opening in 1952.

The Bargain Bank, 1541 Polk Street. Designed by owner Daniel Kahn in collaboration with Wet Studios in 1999, the armored truck seen crashing into the building and spilling its loot symbolizes the bargain prices to be found in this general-merchandise store. The truck is a painted wood-cut profile, and the bills are enlarged replicas applied to the building so that they flutter in the wind.

Stogies, 2801 Jones Street. Based on a conception by store owner Mark Stone, it was the first three-dimensional work by Back to the Drawing Board. The tip of the cigar lights up at night.

Left. Stogies, 2801 Jones Street. The mural was painted by K. Dyble Thompson in 1997. It was commissioned by owner Mark Stone when he saw some of her work on the sidewalk during an "art challenge" held in the Anchorage shopping area, where the store is located. Ready to leave town, Ms. Thompson agreed to stay on an extra week to complete the portraits of George Burns, Marilyn Monroe, and Groucho Marx, seen here in a detail from the mural, and the artist hasn't been spotted in San Francisco since.

Katz Bagels, 3004 16th Street. Owner Mike Katz wanted a new sign for his business and con-
sulted Back to the Drawing Board, which had been trying for years to talk storeowners into using a
spaceship. The UFO bagel, piloted by a friendly green alien, is an ambitious and challenging project carved from foam set over a metal skeleton, polyurethaned, and decorated with 329 simulated
sesame seeds. It started zooming in 1999.

Truly Mediterranean, 1724 Haight Street. The owner commissioned Jon Weiss in 1997 to paint
Middle Eastern scenes in the interior as well as on the front of his restaurant.

Blue Front Cafe, 1430 Haight Street. This spirited genie was designed by Back to the Drawing Board in 1999 to advertise the restaurant's Middle Eastern cuisine.

Left. Art Explosion, 2425 17th Street. This block-long warehouse houses gallery space for a group of independent artists. The mural was funded by The City four years ago as part of an anti-graffiti campaign.

Berkeley Farms, 2065 Oakdale Avenue. The galvanized-metal replicas of the company's milk cartons were installed in 1970.

Molecule, 433 South Van Ness Avenue. Owner Wilson Murray made this sign to show that he sells "anything and everything," including collectibles, artifacts, unusual garden products, and ornamentation. The spider was a Halloween decoration two years ago and remains because the neighbors liked it.

Sparky's Vintage Clothing, 1732 Haight Street. The custom-made, one-of-a-kind rocket ship was modeled on vintage toys, and the lettering style was taken from a 1950s serial, *Raider Men of the Moon*. "Sparky," the robot, was designed and built by owner Das Anastasiou, who opened the vintage-clothing store in 1996.

Overleaf. Black Cat Café, 501 Broadway. The wall with simulated graffiti was created by abstract painter Ray Stevens in collaboration with graffiti artist Toph One. It is based on Lawrence Ferlinghetti's poem "Not too long . . ." published in *Pictures of the Gone Wind* (1956). The restaurant is in North Beach, which is generally regarded as the home of the Beatnik movement.

Magnolia Pub and Brewery, 1398 Haight Street. The sign, painted on the side of the building, contains a beer keg poking through the wall. It was conceived by owner David McLean in collaboration with freelance-artist Jon Weiss, who lives in the neighborhood and has done other storefront work on Haight Street. The pub features original beers brewed on the premises.

Sutter Fine Foods, 988 Sutter Stre. Back to the Drawing Board wanted to suggest the magical sandwiches that the owner could prepare. A portrait of the owner is included in the luscious sidewalk advertisement collage.

Lupanns, 4072 18th Street. Sinfully delicious food served by an angel, as envisioned by Back to the Drawing Board. The restaurant is closed, but the sign remains.

Tricolore Cafe and Pizzeria, 590 Washington Street. Back to the Drawing Board created another heavenly body offering food, which emerges from the green, white, and red of the Italian flag.

Pizza Orgasmica, 3157 Fillmore Street. The name of the restaurant, whose slogan is "We never fake it," was the idea of owner Taylor Maia. Back to the Drawing Board decided to revamp the biblical account of Adam and Eve and have Adam tempt Eve with a slice of pizza.

California Wine Harvest, 2800 Leavenworth Street. Done by Back to the Drawing Board in 1998, this chic, bibulous couple is sharing each other's wine.

Overleaf. Pizzelle, 314 Columbus Avenue. Owner Sam Sard wanted a "boy meets girl" theme for his Italian restaurant, which attracts a young crowd and stays open until 4 a.m. in the bustling North Beach neighborhood. An Italian restaurant has been here for sixty years. The sign was painted by Carlos Perdez, who did additional work inside.

Clean Living, 3141 Fillmore Street. Done by Back to the Drawing Board in 1992, this is an example of their penchant for take-offs on famous fairy tales and literary characters. It is perhaps the only instance where the lamb gets equal billing with the wolf.

Spencer Smyth Galleries, 495 Jackson Street. The figure is taken from a famous Maurin Quina tonic-water poster by Leonetto Cappiello, with the scrolls substituted for the bottle.

Curly's, 1624 Powell Street. Owner Yoko Maeda had used a picture of her husband dressed in a traditional Oriental robe as a logo for years; now updated and animated by Back to the Drawing Board, the figure symbolizes the Asian touch given to American food.

Rococoa's Faerie Queene Chocolates, 415 Castro Street. The Faerie Queene, the idea of owner Jeoffrey Douglas based on Edmund Spenser's lengthy poem of the same name, was made in 1991 by Sennett Gauche, who also did sculpture and paintings for the interior.

Thos. E. Cara, Ltd., 517 Pacific Avenue. This family-owned espresso-machine business has been in the same North Beach location since 1963. Owner Christopher Cara wanted to resolve the graffiti problem on an alley wall next to the store. And after interviewing a number of candidates from the San Francisco Art Institute picked Jason Henry Wasiak to paint a replica of the 1920s La Pavoni machine on display in the shop. The spilled coffee was the artist's idea, who describes himself as being multifaceted. He does illustration, set design, conceptual/installation sculpture, and performance art where he engages an audience with a live-action presentation. He is influenced by conceptual-performance artist Vito Acconci.

Anchorage Ice Cream, 333 Jefferson Street. Created by Back to the Drawing Board in 1997, using their favorite flavors.

Cool Doggy-O's, 468 Green Street. The store is closed, but the sign remains.

Sox Sox Sox, 2801 Leavenworth Street. Sculpted from stone by Ken Guin. The present owner adopted the cats made for a previous business (the twin is on the other side of the door) when he opened his sock-and-gift store five years ago.

San Francisco Sports, 2800 Leavenworth Street. This largest pair of running shoes in San Francisco was carved out of foam by Back to the Drawing Board, and includes forty feet of plastic laces, which light up at night.

NOTES

[1]Arthur Frommer, *Guide to San Francisco, 1987-8* (Prentice Hall Press, New York, 1987), p. 140.

[2]R.W. Sexton, *American Commercial Buildings of Today* (Architectural Book Publishing Company, New York, 1928), p. 156.

[3]William Green, *The Retail Store* (Van Nostrand Reinhold Company, New York, 1986), p. vii.

[4]Vilma Barr and Charles E. Broudy, *Designing to Sell* (McGraw-Hill Book Company, New York, 1986), p. 151.

[5]Martin M. Pegler, editor, *Storefronts and Facades, Book 2* (Retail Reporting Corporation, New York, 1988), pp. 53-54.

[6]Vilma Barr and Charles E. Broudy, *Designing to Sell* (McGraw-Hill Book Company, New York, 1986), p. 175.

[7]Arthur Chandler, editor, *Old Tales of San Francisco* (Kendall/Hunt Publishing Company, Dubuque, Iowa, 1977), pp. 112-113.

[8]Geoffrey Moorhouse, *San Francisco* (Time-Life Books, Amsterdam, 1979), p. 100.

[9]Richard D. Heffner, editor, *Alexis de Tocqueville, Democracy in America* (Mentor Books, New York, 1950), pp. 11, 215, 270-272.

[10]San Francisco Chamber of Commerce, *San Francisco Guidebook, 1915* (San Francisco, 1915), p. 3.

[11]Clarence E. Edwards, *Bohemians in San Francisco* (Paul Elder and Company, San Francisco, 1914), p. 6.

[12]Geoffrey Moorhouse, *San Francisco* (Time-Life Books, Amsterdam, 1979), p. 125.

[13]Thomas Albright, *Art in the San Francisco Bay Area, 1945-1980* (University of California Press, Los Angeles, 1985), pp. xv-xvi.

[14]Herbert Gold, *Travels in San Francisco* (Arcade Publishing, New York, Little Brown Company, 1990), p. 4.

[15]*San Francisco Chronicle*, September 21, 1999, p. A3.

[16]Martin M. Pegler, editor, *Storefront and Facades, Book 1* (Retail Reporting Corporation, New York, 1986), p. 7.

[17]*Ibid.*, Book 2, p. 97.

[18]William Green, *The Retail Store* (Van Nostrand Reinhold Company, New York, 1986), p. 66.